The BRIGHT SIDE of a BROKEN HEART

a memoir   MICHELLE D'AVELLA

Library of Congress Control Number: 2017953507

ISBN-13: 978-1975656867
ISBN-10: 1975656865
1st Edition, September 2017

Printed in the United States of America

For my mother,
whose relentless love and support
has been the foundation of my life.

CONTENTS

TOOLS FOR YOUR JOURNEY

Pushing Beauty

This is my virtual home where I share in-depth articles, workshops, and teachings on healing. Head over there to explore more: www.pushingbeauty.com.

Social Sharing

Use the hashtag #TheBrightSide while you read the book or document your own healing journey. Follow me on Instagram: @pushingbeauty.

Grieving Hearts Club

While I was mourning, I wanted nothing more than to connect with other heartbroken people, but I didn't know where to go or how to find them. To help others in need of support, I created a private Facebook group. Learn how to join at www.pushingbeauty.com/thebrightside.

Breathwork for the Brokenhearted

A virtual workshop led by me where you'll be guided through Breathwork and given prompts to use your heartbreak to learn and grow. Use this course to open your heart, uncover your worth, and release your pain: www.pushingbeauty.com/thebrightside.

HI FRIEND.

I'm going to call you friend because we're about to get incredibly close. Inside the first few pages of this book you'll be with me, at the lowest point of my life, when I was crippled on the bathroom floor, heart splattered beside me. It's not my most glamorous of moments, but it's human, and I have come to love all of what it means to be human.

Here's the thing: I didn't really want to write this story. I would have much rather told the tale of finding myself through a lens other than my broken heart. I didn't have much choice, though. My soul pulled me to this story over and over again. Many times I resisted. Often, I resented the tears from reliving it.

But the truth is that writing this story has been a tremendous part of my healing. Heartbreak reveals all of our deepest fears, all of the beliefs we've tried our best to forget we've accepted as truth.

Writing this story has helped me discover that sometime, too early in life, I decided that I wanted to be loved more than I wanted to be me. And I decided that being me was not worth loving.

This healing journey has also reawakened early childhood memories, when I was pulled toward things no one else around me was interested in. I can see now that in those times my soul was showing me the way forward. It was saying, "Go. Explore. Discover who you are."

It took me most of my 33 years to fully sit in the truth that I have been terrified to get to know who I really am. I didn't trust that I could love all of those parts of me, especially the parts I had pushed away. I didn't trust that the Universe would support me.

But now I know the truth: that there could never be anything I uncover that is not lovable.

In these pages you will find my journey through what looks like a broken heart but turns out to be a dark night of the soul. I didn't know what I was signing up for when I committed to healing, but I knew it was time.

You might be feeling the same way now. If so, my greatest hope is that these words will spark in you the courage and desire to walk through your own pain and allow it to transform you.

No matter where you find yourself on this path, the truth

is: you are always loved, deserving of love, and worthy of being here.

With love,
Michelle D'Avella
May 11, 2017

DEAR FORMER LOVE OF MINE,

Your absence gave me the opportunity to discover myself, an enormous feat each of us must do alone. This journey spanned the breadth of human emotion, took me through the darkest cavern and into the brightest light. It was a ride I never would have chosen on my own, and it couldn't have been more perfect. What has felt like ages of wrinkled time has brought me to this sacred truth: in every single shard of glass is a Milky Way of love.

Your heart may never feel how much I loved you, but I trust that your soul knows.

There will always be traces of you in me.

In gratitude,
Michelle D'Avella
December 20, 2016

INTROD

UCTION

WE ARE STARDUST

One summer, a few years ago, my family and I pulled old comforters out of closets and plopped ourselves under the meteor shower in our backyard. Between sips of red wine we *Ooohed* and *Aaahed* as each chunk of rock burst into light and disintegrated.

There is beauty in every ending.

WHEN
STO

TIME

PS

I'M LIKE A GRIEVING COW

It may sound pathetic, depending on your recent rumbling with grief and your capacity for empathy, but I envision myself like a pained animal.

I once read a true story about a cow whose calf was taken from her womb and shipped out to be sold and slaughtered. She wailed and wailed in the agony of her loss. I've never had a child, but my pain reminds me of hers. The sudden loss of love with no warning.

She never saw it coming, and neither did I.

INTRODUCING: THE MAGICIAN

I thought blindsiding breakups were for people who didn't pay attention, for people who were somewhat *choosing* to be blind. Now I know that some people are really good at hiding the truth—even from themselves.

The story goes like this: We were in love. We were best friends. We were planning a life together. We were happy (or so it seemed). Apparently warning signals weren't his style. There was no smoke before he told me he felt like he was disappearing.

And then he disappeared.

THE BATHROOM FLOOR
IS MY ALLY

I'm curled up on the bathroom floor. My back leaning against the tub, wet hair wrapped in a towel, feet cramped against the wall.

He left me about an hour ago.

I'm hiding in the bathroom because the other rooms are too filled with light, too much a reminder of life. I get in the shower after he leaves because I don't know what else to do. I sob, crouched on the tub floor as the hot water rains down on me.

I switch the faucet to cold once I realize I am numb.

GRIEF IS STALKING ME

My brother happens to call me in the middle of my bathroom floor mourning. He suggests I fly to New York City to spend a few days with him. I don't know how I make it there but the next morning I'm sitting in LAX, tears streaming down my face as I wait to board my flight.

Grief is not discerning. It follows me through the airport, sits down with me for dinner, joins me on my yoga mat, helps itself into the homes of friends, and accompanies me in my car. It is a weight that accumulates until it becomes so heavy that sobbing is my only relief.

I couldn't care less what anyone thinks of me. Someone has walked away with my heart.

All self concern has left with them.

NO
ESCA

PING ME

MAKE A BREAK FOR IT

I am numb, staring out the window at 39,000 feet, when I begin to plan my escape. It's clear that I can't live in the place I call home. His energy is all up in everything, and to make matters worse he lives down the street. We shop at the same grocery store. We practice yoga at the same studio. All signs obviously point to:

Move.

I imagine myself everywhere but Los Angeles. In my mind I roam the streets of Philadelphia, New York, San Francisco, San Diego, even Portland and Austin.

I'm disappointed by the feeling of these cities in my daydream. They are dark and gloomy, rainclouds looming overhead. I begin to submit to the fact that while he would not reside in these places, I would.

And I am the place the pain lives.

BROTHERLY LOVE

It's 10pm when I land at JFK. My brother picks me up, and we drive to Brooklyn. Some of my favorite hip-hop songs from the 90s fill the tiny, dimly lit Japanese restaurant where we've decided to grab a late dinner.

Sitting across from my brother, one of my best friends, reminds me that I am loved. I belong somewhere. This person has been in my life since the day he was born. He isn't going anywhere.

I can feel slivers of anxiety begin to dissipate. In the presence of home I start to feel like I can land, like there is safe ground after all.

It helps anchor me in a time when I feel like I could just float away.

YOU CAN RUN BUT
YOU CAN'T HIDE

I don't "wake up" the next morning. That action is reserved for people who sleep. My eyes simply open. I hear the sounds of cars moving and people laughing. I have forgotten that joy exists, and I wonder what I would be doing this Sunday morning if I had my life back.

My mind is stuck on replay, obsessively looping the last conversation with my ex. *Ex.* God, I can't believe I'm using that word to refer to the person I believed I would be spending the rest of my life with. The thought makes my heart feel like it's coming up my throat.

I'm saddened to realize that repositioning myself 3,000 miles east of Los Angeles does not make my heart ache any less.

MAYBE, BABY

My mind and heart are at odds. My heart is trying to mourn, but my mind is convinced that this isn't the end. That this is his depression talking. That there is no way I could be this blindsided by someone I spent most of my waking (and un-waking) hours with.

I want to side with my mind, even if that thread of hope is as sturdy as spider's silk. I stare at my phone and refresh my email every couple of minutes, as if I can will him into regret. It's not working so I cave in and email him. Instead of wearing the mask of bravery he is used to seeing from me, I let my dying heart speak.

He replies several hours later that he doesn't have any words. He is also crumbling, his heart breaking.

He seems to be just as confused as I am.

THANK GOODNESS
FOR PEOPLE

I take the bus to my childhood home in New Jersey and fall into my mother's arms. I spend time with people who have always been there: my siblings, my parents, my cousins, my best friend.

I sleep in the room I grew up in, the room I have mourned lost friendships, missed opportunities, and lives gone too soon. It is in this room that I have laid with myself through so much of life's sweetness and devastation.

I lay awake at night staring at the glow-in-the-dark stars the twelve-year-old version of me strategically placed on the ceiling twenty years ago. I feel really grateful that I am so loved.

Everywhere I look, people are around me, catching me as I fall.

A GLIM OF

MER
HOPE

THE EMPTY KISS

I'm back in Los Angeles, and there is a moment of hope for us. It slips away again, and he spends the night holding me while I soak his shirt with my tears. I sob for hours, and he is kind enough to soothe me.

As he strokes my hair I wonder how little he wants to be here with me. Only a few days ago he squeezed me tightly, lovingly calling me, "Baby, baby…" and now his touch feels obligatory.

I keep asking the same questions. He is trying to give me answers, I know, but he doesn't know how. Or maybe his responses just don't satisfy me.

When he leaves, I kiss his lips. I think we are having this tragic moment of love parting ways.

But his lips don't move.

NO TRACE LEFT BEHIND

This is the second time he leaves, and I know it's for good. I feel like I've lost my mind so I wander around the apartment trying to find it.

Instead I find his residue:
Photos of our life covering the side of the fridge.
Beautiful love notes in his handwriting.
A framed photograph from our trip to Mexico.
A toothbrush.
One sock.
A stack of books his mom lent me.
A cheese grater.
Kimchi in the fridge.

I stay up all night combing the apartment until I'm confident there isn't a trace left of him anywhere. In the morning my friend drives me down the street where I leave a bag of our mementos hanging on his doorknob.

The next week, when I finally use my car, I glance over to see his knee brace in the passenger seat.

I get out and throw it in the trash.

I'VE

FAL

AND I CA

LEN

N'T GET UP

NOTHING CAN BE UNDONE

My spirit is lost. There is a soft residue of ash holding space for the part of me that loves life. She is gone, and I don't know if she will ever return. For the first time in my life I don't care if she does.

Each beat of my shredded heart pushes salt water to my eyes. My face is forever stained. My pillow is eternally soggy. My bed holds fast the warm indentation of my body. My heart endlessly aches.

I know I will never be the same.

LET THE MOURNING BEGIN

I have hope that sleep can be my savior, a safe place for me to drift away from my pain. But I'm too afraid of remembering again so I stay awake for over 40 hours.

I resort to inviting good ol' Mary J. in to help me drift off. She ushers me into dreams, but every few hours I wake up with tears streaming down my face before I even know why.

Nothing I do comes close to making anything feel better. And so I realize I am not meant to feel better right now.

I am meant to feel what it means to deeply mourn.

120 POUNDS TO FREEDOM

Along with sleep, my appetite vanishes, and my jeans start sagging. I once loved food. Now it makes me nauseous. I force myself to nibble on toast. It ends up glaring at me from a plate most of the day.

I only move when I really have to. Like when my mom calls to tell me I need to make a smoothie. Or when I have to pee.

Moving is too hard. It feels like I'm lugging a body around.

I really just want to be free.

THE SUN IS SHINING
& I WANT TO DIE

One morning I wake up, and I don't know how to get out of bed. I call my mom, and she doesn't answer. I call my friend, and she doesn't answer. I feel utterly alone, and fear overwhelms me.

I think I should feel the sun on my skin so I force myself to go for a walk. I feel my feet moving. The sun warms my face. I look up to the trees to find the appreciation I once easily found in life.

Nothing is there.

I won't do anything about it, but I really don't want to be here anymore. Tears stream down my cheeks from behind my sunglasses. I keep walking. I want to die, but I don't.

I keep walking.

I keep living.

EMBERS OF OPTIMISM
TURNED TO SOOT

A man I once dated called me an eternal optimist. It felt true at the time. But as I lay here staring at the ceiling, tears silently pouring from my eyes, it's clear to me that couldn't have been me.

I am someone who cries all day, every day. I am someone who seems to have lost all zest for life. I am someone who can't even find hope in sunshine.

I don't want to be the abandoned woman losing all care for life because of a man.

But Goddammit, apparently I am.

AN ARSON ON THE LOOSE

I hold close to my heart the belief that I want him back. One day I imagine him knocking on my door, regret in his eyes and remorse on his face. In this daydream I feel my heart sinking as I recognize that I can never take him back. I don't actually want a relationship with this man.

What I really want is to un-know what I now know. I want to go back to what felt safe and cozy. But now I know that he is not the one for me. His leaving is showing me more about him than he ever allowed me to see in his presence.

This recognition does not lessen the aching of my heart, but it helps me see the truth. This is done. He lit fire to our home and fled.

There is nothing left to come back to.

FORGIVENESS MAKES ME
WANT TO THROW UP

I crawl out of bed long enough to visit a friend for tea. She tells me that when her last relationship ended she committed to a three-month meditation honoring her ex each morning.

This idea sounds beautiful to me. I love him. I want the best for him. I want to set him free. More importantly, this feels like something I can actually do to move this healing process along.

So I wake up the next morning, sit up to meditate, and I imagine him in front of me. But instead of feeling love, I want to vomit. My body rejects everything about this.

I decide to focus on giving myself love instead. I feel my body relax. I listen to its wisdom.

There is no rushing healing.

THE WORDS OF WISE WOMEN

This grief feels like eternity. It feels so unbearably crushing that there is no chance it could ever feel lighter. In these moments I cling to five words my friend Katherine shares with me. They are words given to her while she mourned a devastating breakup, and she passes the wisdom on to me:

This is just for now.

I let the words sink into my heart. They remind me that our entire lives are a series of moments that move from light to dark and back to light again.

Everything is always changing.

THE GHOST OF GRIEF

Some time has passed. I'm not sure how much. Somehow things seem to get done, but I don't know how.

Laundry is clean. Food is made, and it appears my body has begun to eat again. I drive to yoga and reply to emails. My mouth opens and words come out.

I don't know how, but life keeps moving, and somehow I'm moving with it.

THE
UNIV
IS TALKI

ERSE

NG TO ME

LOOK A LITTLE
CLOSER, DARLING

In the moments when I'm not completely consumed with hurt I become obsessed with solving this puzzle. I desperately need to know what I did to make him leave. I'm convinced I must have been unbearable, and I reflect on all of the ways I could have been a better partner.

This willingness to see my flaws is valuable. I discover important things that will help me become a more compassionate, loving human. But I don't see anything that proves the way I feel: unlovable.

Leave-able.

I begin to let in the truth that maybe his leaving says more about him than it does about me.

And maybe my pain is more about me than it is about him.

YOU ARE BEING CLEARED OUT

On what would have been our anniversary, I decide I should do something good for myself, something healing. I book a massage and whisper to the masseuse my warning, "I'm going through a breakup so I might be crying."

She nods, smiles, and gently squeezes my arm.

I do cry. Softly. Quietly. I don't want to disturb her.

Afterward she walks me to the doorway, turns, and moves her hands in giant sweeping strokes around my body as if to brush my pain away. When she's done she grabs my shoulders, looks into my eyes, and says, "You are being cleared out for something better to come in."

I smile through tears. Somewhere deep inside I know she is right.

TOLD YA SO

The following week I teach a Breathwork workshop. The last thing I want to do is have anyone looking to me for support, but as soon as we begin I feel like I am exactly where I need to be. I feel purposeful, and I am reminded that this is the work I have been called to do with my life.

After the class one of my students gives me a giant hug. She squeezes my shoulders, looks into my eyes, and says, "Thank you. You are doing something so important for people. Maybe right now your job isn't to give love to someone else. Maybe right now your job is just to love you. You're being cleared out, honey. Something bigger and better is coming your way."

I drive home with my head held a little higher. I hear you, Universe.

I hear you.

AT THE
THE RO
SIGN THA
ENO

END OF

AD IS A

T READS

UGH

LOST ON BARREN LAND

I call my mom every day, often several times a day. Sometimes when she answers she hears nothing but muffled sobs. My connection with her helps me remember I am anchored to someone, that there is a reason to be alive.

Even though we are both rooting for me to pick myself up and find myself again, I can't seem to figure out how to begin. I feel like I've been tossed off a truck in the middle of the desert and left to find my way home.

I see no tracks in the dirt or sign posts anywhere. The sky is always cloudy. There are no stars to guide me. I hear my mother's voice in the distance, calling me forward.

But I can't tell where it's coming from.

THIS JOURNEY BELONGS TO YOU, HONEY

There is a moment on the road through grief and despair when everything changes. A friend of mine encountered this moment laying in a pool of her own vomit. Mine comes when I ask my mother to come stay with me and she feeds me four of the most loving words she can:

I. Can't. Save. You.

Tears of recognition stream from the corners of my eyes, following a riverbed back behind my ears. A voiceless scream of, "Enough."

IT'S TIME WHEN IT'S TIME

Enough is not a mustering up of strength to get on with life. It is not disgust and disgrace with myself. It is my welcome sign that reads: "Enough Resisting." It's time to face what you've been hiding from.

I look down at my body and see that my arms have been extended, silently reaching, begging to be rescued.

Relief washes over me as I realize that I can save myself.

THE
BOT

TOM

BREATHE ME BACK TO LIFE

When I was younger and didn't know how to heal myself, I hardened to stone. My warmth evaporated and my emotions felt far from reach. Numb felt normal until I was ready to feel again.

That's when I discovered Breathwork, and my life changed. My breath has shown me the truth time and time again. It has connected me to my soul, it has healed my wounds, and it has opened my heart.

So now I know I have to begin doing the work that taught me how to love myself in the first place.

It's time to fall into the darkness and find out where it will take me.

INTO THE CAVE, BAT WOMAN

The depression is not The Bottom. Crying in endless waves is not The Bottom. Lack of care for my own life is not The Bottom. Those places are aimless meanderings of grief. They are a lost vessel with empty eyes, but not The Bottom.

The Bottom is the place I go when I decide to heal. It is the venturing into the deep well of pain that brings me there. People often talk about Rock Bottom as the place they find themselves and then pull themselves up from.

To me, The Bottom is the place I courageously choose to go. It is the place within us that holds our greatest pain and our greatest fear. It is the scariest, darkest place you will ever venture to.

But it is the only way to heal.

THE RULE

There is no questioning whether or not I've reached The Bottom. It is unmistakable. Fear ripples through every cell of my body, and the pain is overwhelming. Still, I stay.

In this place there is only one rule:

Face the pain or leave.

FEEL IT TO HEAL IT

I lay down to breathe, and it feels like there is an ancient wound opening deep in my core. As I cry, my body heaves repeatedly to purge the pain. My heart feels like it is shattering into a million pieces, and I now know for sure what it means to have a broken heart.

With each breath every barrier I have put up to avoid my pain begins to fall away. I move between breathing, screaming, and crying to release this enormous, heavy energy.

It's hard.

The breathing isn't hard. The screaming isn't hard. The crying isn't hard.

But being with the pain is close to unbearable.

NA-NA-NA-NA-NA
YOU CAN'T SEE ME

My pain begins to show me how completely alone I feel in this life. Even amid loving family and friends, I feel like no one really sees me. Like no one can love me the way I need to be loved. Like I don't belong anywhere. Like I never have. Like maybe being here is a mistake.

The pain of these beliefs engulf me, my rational brain shuts off, and it hurts so much that I literally believe I am going to die.

But I don't run from it anymore. I stay firm and surrender to the pain.

I feel, but I don't die.

THE JOURNEY HOME

There is no gold yet, but somewhere, buried deep under the pain, cracks of light start to come in. It doesn't happen all the time, but when it does it carries in truth and love. These moments privilege me to the clarity of the false beliefs imprisoning my heart.

I am discovering that The Bottom is the beginning of the journey, not the end. It turns out I have many pieces to pick up along the way.

THE
STRU
IS
RE

GGLE
AL

WEAKNESS: IT'S A-OKAY

I've been on this self-love road for a while, so my mind is smart enough to tell me all of the things I need to hear. Things like:

Everything is going to be okay.
I'm here for you.
I love you.

But my body feels defeated. It feels weak and heavy and oh-so-sad.

I *am* weak. The last time I saw him he told me I was the strongest person he knows. But I'm not really that strong. I have pretended to be strong all my life because I was afraid of being weak. But now I am weak because I have no strength to pretend.

So I need it to be okay that I am weak. I need to accept that, until now, this kind of vulnerability has been imperceivable to me. Something within me knows that through this weakness I will find true strength.

I'm just not sure when.

I ZIG AND THEN I ZAG

I often have a deep compulsion to take out a needle and thread to sew up the cracks in my heart. I want to strategically and meticulously mend my broken pieces together and sweep up the residue. But, healing doesn't work like that.

I don't face my pain one, two, or three times, and it's over. I don't discover I can safely face my pain and come out the other side a healed woman. I don't see the truth about myself and remember it every moment moving forward. I don't uncover it all in the beginning.

This healing process is messy. I'm going deep. I'm unraveling. There are moments of exasperation and moments of liberation. My spirits lift and fall.

My cousin, Erin, sends me an Instagram post by @frizzkidart. It's an illustration of a flowery line graph moving up and down and up and down again. Beneath it the words say:

Healing is not linear.

STRANGER IN MY HOUSE

Sometimes an ugly energy wraps itself around my vital organs and proclaims my worthlessness. I know that this is not the truth, that I've been hijacked by something that wants to keep me small and meek, frightened and stuck.

During these times I defiantly walk over to the mirror, and through tears, staring directly into my own eyes, I declare my love for myself. I feel no care for the cheesiness of this act because I have a hole in my heart, and only cheesy, pure, gorgeous self-love can fill it.

When sorrow and shame wash over me instead of sleep at night, I say to myself, "I love you, Michelle." I repeat this mantra over and over again until I believe it enough to fall asleep.

PERMISSION TO BE DRUGGED

I have gathered up enough care for life to write an article on my blog about my heartbreak. I receive beautiful emails from people who are finding solace in my vulnerability and who are reminding me of the strength in my weakness.

People also email me to give me permission to medicate myself. Some of my friends and family do the same. I'm not entirely sure if they are trying to help me or themselves. We are a culture that fears pain regardless who it belongs to.

These suggestions frustrate me. My soul is asking for nothing more than compassion. A smile, a squeeze, and the simple heartfelt words, "It's okay."

I don't want to hide from this. It's too important. I can feel in my bones that my grief is the appropriate reaction to my current life experience.

I trust that the way out of this pain is not by numbing out, but by feeling it every step of the way.

NOWHERE TO GO,
NO ONE TO BE

Sometimes I slip into the belief that there is some place to get to, a restitution granted only to those who have earned it. I find myself frustrated and resentful. No matter how hard I work, how many tears I shed, or how bright my light shines I can never seem to find the finish line.

When I step outside my victimhood I can see that there is no path and no place to get to. So I scoot over and make some more room for my pain. I stop seeing things as black and white, hot and cold, left and right and begin to recognize that I am the polarities and all the microcosms in between.

There is love even in my darkness.

SPIRITUAL WARRIOR

Life slowly begins to have more moments of laughter, peace, and purpose. I can feel the meaning gradually creeping back in, along with the color in my skin and the meat on my bones.

I am different. I am forever changed. I feel tired and worn down, but at peace.

Like a warrior on her way home.

A SCENE FR

BUT INST

REAL

OM A MOVIE
EAD IT'S
LIFE

THE WORST DOWN DOG
OF MY LIFE

For the first time in months I don't feel that knot of anxiety wrapped tightly in the pit of my stomach. I decide to take a different yoga class than I normally would. I'm one of the first into the room, and I sit in the front row.

We begin with some sitting poses before moving into a flow. Once we get into Down Dog I peer through my legs, my eyes meandering over fingertips gently pressing into rubber mats. They land on a set that are grasping, knuckles slightly bent.

My body recognizes it's him before my mind does. My heart beats fast and loud, reminding me that life can be twisted and unfair.

Just as I'm surfacing he shows up to pull me back under.

JUST LIKE AN
UNANSWERED PRAYER

The class is over, and I'm folded over my hips, forehead pressed to the mat. I am praying. Praying for strength. Or better yet, praying he will get the hint and leave.

He's too nice for that, though. I reluctantly look to my left, and he's there looking down at me with a sweet smile and casual conversation. I'm shaking, and I don't know how to pretend like I'm okay. So I don't.

There are people laughing and talking in the same room as us, but they sound a million miles away. Outside, at my car, I come to terms with the moment and recognize that it's up to me to voice what I need to. I interrupt him after the third time he says, "It's really nice to see you." I say, "It really hurt me to not hear from you at all."

His body clenches up, and time freezes for a moment. Eventually an apology slips through his teeth and then something about getting coffee. I can tell he is lost and that he doesn't know where to go from here. Neither do I.

I turn from him, drive home, fall into bed and cry.

HERE I AM, I EXIST

Two weeks have passed, and there have been no invitations for coffee and no efforts of closure. I decide that his lack of empathy means he doesn't understand, so I decide to shed some light.

The letter is long. I tell him how his actions and lack-there-of have affected me. I tell him what my life has been like in the five months of his absence. I don't ask him to take responsibility for my feelings, but I share them.

I don't realize it yet, but his detachment is not because he doesn't understand. It's because he is choosing not to let it in. He can't handle that he has hurt me.

He doesn't know how to honor my pain.

PAIN TALKS

I write one thing I wish I hadn't. I tell him I would take back every single beautiful moment with him to not have experienced this pain. I write it with conviction. I genuinely mean it at the time. I want him to understand that the pain is so great that it doesn't feel worth any of the love.

Now I know that was the pain talking. The love is always worth it. Real love. And we had some real love. For a moment in time.

He never responds, and we never see each other again.

WAKI
TO W
DES

NG UP

HAT I

ERVE

TAKE ALL OF ME
OR NONE OF ME

I release the ties that wrap my worth to his love. As I free myself, I recognize that I deserve to be with someone who wants 100% of me. Not bits and pieces. Not just the pretty parts, but someone who will embrace all of what makes me human.

I am seeing that all of this pain that's coming up through this breakup are my wounds. I can't blame him for my pain. He has every right to choose what he wants for his life, and he has every right to stop choosing me.

But I don't get to stop choosing myself.

THE ONLY CHOICE

I never want to feel this degree of heartbreak again so I commit to learning from my pain instead of hiding from it. Rather than looking for an easier way out, I face the feelings head on. I breathe as often as I need to. I cry when the sadness surfaces, and if I notice I'm judging myself I knock gently on the door of compassion.

I do this because my soul tells me I have no other choice. I do it for my future self and my future partner, because we deserve to have a beautiful relationship untainted from this trauma.

I'm choosing me because I have to. Because I've tried hiding, and hiding doesn't work for me anymore.

STEPPING UP MY GAME

At the beginning of this breakup I wanted to rush my healing. I wanted to rip the Band-Aid off and, in the blink of an eye, be in love again. I wanted to bypass the most important process of my life.

Now I accept it with patience because I trust love will find me when it's time. I want a deep, unconditional, soul-connected partnership. I'm getting ready for what I once believed I could never have.

That means it's up to me to stop the patterns. It's up to me to raise my vibration. It's up to me to open my heart to let love in. Right now that means I have to be on my own. I have to allow the false beliefs to melt away. I have to stop looking outside myself for someone or something to make me feel better.

It's time to step up and become the best partner of my life.

SEE FEAR, CHOOSE TRUTH

There are times I get so clouded by the feeling of loneliness and sadness that it consumes me. My fear creeps in to have a chat. It tells me I messed it up. It tells me there will be no one else who will love me. It tells me I need to fix it because I will have missed out on my great love.

My soul tells me to chill out. It tells me that everything is perfect exactly as it is. Nothing is missing. Nothing needs to be fixed. I am exactly where I need to be.

I never ask anyone else to fill my void again. In those times of sadness I stay with the feeling and remind myself that the only love that will actually heal this pain is my own.

So I give it to myself.

MINING FOR GOLD

Healing is teaching me so much about life. It's opening my heart up to feel a depth of compassion I've never known. It's teaching me to surrender to all that I am.

I vacillate between highs and lows until I begin to truly accept that feelings are not static. I find solid ground, a new depth opens, and I remember that the earth is always moving, even when we can't feel it.

This process has gradually shifted from healing my broken heart to healing the cracks in my soul. As I begin to delve more deeply into my shadow I am reclaiming my light. I face greater fear than each time before but it's backed with greater strength. I'm not sure where this is leading me but I'm committed to mining, and I know there is no turning back.

I don't yet know I am about to uncover the most important truth of my life.

COM

HO

ING
ME

FOUND: A GIRL IN A COSTUME

Instead of looking to the stars I close my eyes and go deep within. My pain takes me into the belly of the burden I have carried my entire life. There I find a little girl. She is a sweet five year-old with thick brown bangs, sparkling green-blue eyes, and a wild excitement for life.

But she hides in a handmade costume of a lion. In there she feels safe. She thinks no one will see her trembling.

Over time she forgets that she is afraid.

She believes she is the lion.

BRIGHT-EYED BABY

The little girl is here to show me what I have forgotten. She is here to hand me back the parts of myself I have pushed away. She is here to show me that I have been living my life in fear. She is here to teach me that beneath that fear is my true strength.

She leads me back to lost memories and paths unfollowed. She shows me the moments when I sacrificed myself to feel loved.

She is here to show me when I stopped loving myself and why.

GOOD LUCK TO THE GUY

My mom is 20 when she gets pregnant with me, my dad is 26. Like all new parents, they don't know what the hell they are doing, and while they do a pretty good job, no parents are perfect.

I am strong and defiant. They don't know how to handle me. In response my dad often laughs, "Good luck to the guy who ends up with you!"

He says this to me because I am willful. He also says this because I'm not who he thought I would be.

I always dismissed his comment until now.

Now I realize that somewhere along the way I started to believe it.

CHOOSING TO DISAPPEAR

I'm close to ten years old and standing at the desk in my bedroom fiddling with a CD case. I'm contemplating the concept of soulmates and happily-ever-afters.

As quickly as it arrives, my curiosity about who might be out there for me is washed away by a wave of fear. What if God forgot about me? I decide there's not likely to be a man out there who will love me.

This moment, when I decide to believe I am not worthy of being remembered by even God himself, is a mistake. This is a moment that, for no apparent reason, I choose to deny my light. Instead of expanding and allowing my soul to shine, I shrink down and reduce my worth.

I think that if I choose to disappear it won't hurt so badly to be forgotten.

LET'S DO THE TIME WARP

I'm 11 or 12, and time feels as if it's swirling around me and pushing me forward. Things seem to be moving fast, and I feel a deep knowing that this moment is precious, cherish-able.

I share this with one of my closest friends, and she laughs. She has no idea what I'm talking about so she starts teasing me. She shares my feelings with some of our other friends who begin looking at me curiously. It is light and playful. They aren't being malicious.

I laugh with them, but inside I take note that these kinds of thoughts are ones I should keep to myself.

It is the first time in my life when I care more about fitting in than being me.

MEMORIES OF A TWEEN WITCH

My ten-year-old self stands in a floor length white cotton nightgown staring into the mirror at crooked teeth, smirking with excitement. I say Bloody Mary into the mirror three times. Even though nothing happens, I'm satisfied with believing it could.

Ouija boards are a favorite ritual when my cousins come to visit. My mom and I talk about death for hours before bed at night, and I devour stories about ghost encounters. John Edwards frequents my television screen, and I feel ripples move through my body each time an audience member reconnects with a deceased loved one.

None of this ever feels like Hocus Pocus to me, but the world tells me otherwise, and I listen.

Remembering this time feels like discovering remnants of a former life unfulfilled, hidden away, and forgotten.

HELLO, OLD FRIEND

The memories coming to surface feel like I'm bumping into an old friend I haven't seen in years. I call out in exclamation, but she replies with a mixture of hurt and relief, "I've been living in your home all along."

This little girl, excited by mystery, fascinated with death, believer in magic and soulmates—she got shut away long ago. But she didn't go anywhere. She's been within me all along.

She has been waiting for this moment, for someone to show her she belongs.

Now I see that she has been waiting for me.

RECLAM

ATION

THE GREAT SACRIFICE

Now I see that in my relationships I am simultaneously desperate to be seen and loved for who I truly am and terrified that I won't be. The irony is that this fear has kept me from knowing and loving myself.

Each time I feel safe enough to start uncovering the lost parts of myself I smell his fear, and I know he will leave if I move one more inch. "He" shows up in my life in different shapes and personalities. Sometimes he leaves and sometimes he pushes me away, and each time he does, it reaffirms my belief that it's not safe to be me.

In each breakup there is a sacrifice being made to offer me a chance. I am finally taking it.

Now I know I had to lose him to find myself.

THE MOST UN-FUN GAME
TO EVER EXIST

I realize I have been playing a game I don't actually want to play. When I share a part of myself and the world says no I push that part of myself away. I do this over and over again until I think all that's left are the yeses.

What I don't realize is that the nos never go anywhere. Instead, a large part of my energy is spent trying to keep them hidden. I'm always on guard, making sure none of them slip out. Life like this is exhausting.

Instead of being me, I try to mold myself into being who I think I should be, and I push my boyfriends to do the same. I'm so afraid of abandonment that I overlook the fact that I have abandoned myself.

It's true—I am being cleared out for something better to come in.

Me.

THE WHOLLY JOURNEY

I am waking up to the greatest gift of the human journey: discovering who I am. I am reclaiming lost parts of myself that have been stifled and stowed away. Parts that were budding but not fully bloomed.

I am learning to see the false beliefs and live from the truth. I am learning to love the parts of myself I have labeled good *and* bad. I am learning to become wholly me.

It's time to honor the little girl who has been living within me for a lifetime. It's time for her to step out into the world and live as big as she dares.

SEP

GRATITUDE COMES

I wake up to the pitter patter of raindrops falling on my window, a rare and welcome experience in Los Angeles. I get up to make coffee and reach for a mug. My hand lands on a beautiful gift from my ex, one of the only remaining artifacts from our time together. The handcrafted ceramic glazed in desert hues was my favorite coffee cup, one that has gotten little use the last few months.

As I pull it toward me a sense of clarity and gratitude washes over me. I don't have to sit down to meditate. I don't have to imagine him in front of me. My mind does not take me to this place, my heart does.

I don't linger on him. It's a brief moment of feeling love and contentment for everything that has come before, everything that is here now, and everything that is working its way to me.

I can't imagine my life any different, and in this moment I feel how much I have healed.

I AM NOT SHINY

I have tried to be shiny most of my life. I have buried away the parts of myself that felt rusty and unlovable. I have perpetuated the false belief that it's not okay to be messy, that I will be abandoned in my vulnerability, that weakness is too risky, and that trying to be someone I think I should be will get me what I want.

The truth is that I am not shiny. I'm messy, and now I'm okay with that. I like that I'm human. I like that the process is not perfect. I like that I can surrender to the imperfections and let the right people flow in and out of my life. I like that I can allow myself to feel pain and joy in a single day. I like that I can choose to heal myself.

I am not shiny. I am patina. I am worn and lived.

Just like someone who has loved and lost.

OUR SOULS KNOW

There is a part of me that knows everything is beautiful. I love him and he loves me, and we will never be again. And it's perfectly fine. And he knows it's fine. And we don't have to have any words together to know it's fine.

And at the same time there is a part of me that is still a little bit heartbroken that there was no looking in the eye, no honoring, no heartfelt apology for immense pain.

I know he never wanted to break my heart.

But he still did.

ONE YEAR LATER

As I write this story there are times I am still brought to tears. The tears are different, though. They are wise old woman tears. Each drop is full of a knowing, an appreciation, and a surrendering.

Now my pain is not about him. It's about me. In truth, it's always been about me. But now, even though it's wrapped in gratitude, my heart still hurts for the pain I endured. The tragedy of the way it all fell apart.

I wish I could say he and I made amends, that we love and respect one another and wish each other nothing but the best.

The truth is that sometimes we don't get to have it all wrapped up with a bow.

EVERYONE IS JOURNEYING

The man I once loved is a beautiful human being. I know nothing of his life since we parted, but I still know that. It's why I loved him so dearly. He has his reasons for leaving, and I trust they are ones that served his own life. I know they have ended up serving mine.

As I've said, this story isn't really about him. But of course that's not entirely true. The lessons I've learned from this experience are ones that relate to me, but they wouldn't have shown up in my life in this way if not for him.

We affect one another. The way we treat each other matters. It has a lasting impact. Also, we aren't perfect. In the words of Ram Dass, "We're all just walking each other home."

So while this breakup had a tremendous impact on my life, it had its own effect on his. We are each on our own journey. Even without squeaky clean closure, I'm glad he was in mine for the short time he was.

THE
BRIGH
OF A
BRO

TSIDE

KEN

HEART

PH.D. IN PAIN

There is nothing wrong with me because I feel pain. In fact, the more I fight my pain or try to numb it out, the more it controls me. My fear of pain has kept me out of love. It has kept me small. It has pushed people away. It has manifested my greatest fears. Most importantly, it has kept me from knowing myself.

My pain has served me greatly. It has taught me so much about myself, and for this I am forever grateful. It has guided me into my fear and sadness to show me what I've been hiding from and who I really am.

I don't run from my pain anymore. I don't make it a problem. I don't judge it or call it weak. I allow it to have a voice. I see it for what it is: information.

And I use it to keep healing.

WAKING UP TO MAGIC

This breakup blew up all my fears. It cleared everything out so I no longer had anything to lose. The last threads hanging on to staying small were cut, and I was left face-to-face with the unbearable pain of the truth.

Except that it turns out it *is* bearable. It's not *comfortable*. It's not easy. It has put my nose to the face of death and left my cells vibrating with fear. It has kicked up the dust, left me humbled and shaken.

It has also taught me that I can face anything. I can handle anything. Now I know that my strength was hidden by fear and that fear is nothing to be afraid of.

Deciding to heal, to face my pain and see the truth, is the best choice I have ever made.

ON THE OTHER SIDE

The pain is not entirely gone, but I am already new. In those first moments I began to face the pain I became new. As I surrender to my pain I release more of the construct of who I thought I was and become more of who I have been afraid to be.

On the other side I find myself embracing the messiness of life. On the other side I find the truth that the highest highs and lowest lows are all the same beauty inherent in this life. On the other side I see that it's all really one thing: love.

In showing up to do this work, I have reclaimed parts of myself that were lost long ago and released parts that were no longer serving me. On the other side of this broken heart I am strong and powerful. I am forever changed and more myself than I have ever been.

And that is worth everything.

THE

IS

BEGIN

END
THE
NING

I PUT A HEX ON YOU...OR NOT

Healing is a process. As I've heard my teacher say, "Sometimes grief can be like a dent in the fender that never goes away." There are moments, from time to time, when I release some more grief from this breakup. It hides away in the nooks and crannies of my bones.

Sometimes I still imagine bumping into my ex. Some days I see myself smiling joyfully at him, feeling what I imagine we all feel for each other when we die—nothing but love.

Other times I glare at him like I'm Cruella de Vil. I wish to know witchy things so I can cast a spell on him and make him suffer forever.

These are split second moments. They are silly little thoughts, but they point to the truth that the pain isn't all gone. Even as much as I love myself. Even as much as I don't want him as my partner. Even as thankful as I am that we are no longer together.

Hurt is still in there somewhere.

JUST AS IT IS

I am not incomplete without a partner. My life is not any less worth living. My joy is not remotely diminished. I don't pine for my new love to come in, but I welcome him at any time.

I love who I am. I love the life I've created. I love my friends, my family, my clients, my students, my teachers, and my guides. I love the work I do and the way I choose to spend my time. I love this Earth, and my adventures through it.

When my partner shows up he will bring even more love, even more joy, and even more depth to my life. But I am not any less in the meantime. I'm showing up the best I can every single moment, and for the first time in my life I truly feel whole. Lovable. Deserving of an incredible partnership.

And I trust it will show up exactly when it needs to.

A STORY REWROTE

There is no squeaky clean, happily ever ending. This book is not instructions, a step-by-step process to heal your heart. The truth is that healing is messy. There is no guide. You just need to keep showing up. You face the pain. You make difficult choices in life to support what you deserve.

Things get better. And if you really put in the work, if you release the idea that you're a victim, and instead choose to surrender to all of who you are, things get way better.

I don't need to be in love to feel love. I don't need to have a sit down with my ex to be healed. Everything I need is within me. And from there I know I can create all that I want.

THROUGH HOOPS OF FIRE

This past year has been the most difficult of my life. It has also been the most rewarding. I keep showing up in ways that surprise me, and each time my life swells with a little more love.

I lead groups and help people move through their own pain. I waste less and less energy on things that don't serve me, and I spend what I've saved doing my soul's work.

I know who I am. I know what is meant for me. I am more interested in being authentic than in being perfect, more interested in healing than in hiding, more interested in knowing what is right for me than in filling a void with not-quite-right love.

This beautiful life emerged from the heart splattered devastation on my bathroom floor. And I would go through all of the pain I experienced a million times over to become who I am now.

THANK YOU

THE BRIGHT SIDE

Thank you for being a part of this journey with me. If you're interested in working together, I offer:

1:1 healing and mentoring sessions
Virtual and in-person workshops
A self-led heartbreak healing workshop
A free Facebook support group
Articles and teachings on healing

If you commit to healing, I'm confident you will find the bright side.

Learn more about working with me at
www.pushingbeauty.com/thebrightside

Connect With Me
Website: pushingbeauty.com
Instagram: @pushingbeauty
Facebook: pushingbeautynow
Twitter: @michelledavella

SO GRATEFUL

I am blessed to be supported by so many wonderful people. It feels appropriate to name a few who helped me bring this book to life.

Endless gratitude goes out to my teacher and mentor, David Elliott, whose love, support, and guidance allowed me to honor this book as a portal for my own healing.

Melissa Stephenson, your attention to detail, big picture perspective, and grammatical wisdom helped polish and refine my baby. Thank you deeply for your support.

Thank you to my first readers: Mom, Brett, Morgan, Madison, and Megan. To my brother Matt, thank you for your encouragement and support in the final design phases. I am so thankful for the love and support of my entire family, each member who is a dear friend.

Mom and Dad, thank you for your constant love and support and for always encouraging me to explore what feels true to me.

ABOUT MICHELLE D'AVELLA

Michelle D'Avella is a writer, Breathwork teacher, and spiritual mentor. Her mission is to inspire people to take ownership of their lives through emotional and spiritual healing.

Through her 1:1 programs, group workshops, and self-led courses, Michelle teaches her students how to release pain, uncover truth, and create a new relationship to life. She lives in Los Angeles and works with clients all over the world.

Her writing has been published on The Huffington Post, MindBodyGreen, TinyBuddha, and Elephant Journal. Her work has been featured in W Magazine, Covetuer, MyDomaine and others.

@pushingbeauty
www.pushingbeauty.com
Facebook: pushingbeautynow

Printed in Great Britain
by Amazon